Dear Ms. Hall S0-BDR-247
We appreciate the gifts
you are teaching our
son. Under your
guidance he has
expanded his horizons
through knowledge
of Language Arts
and Social Studies.
Your efforts to teach
Jacob and his peers
will result in a
world full of hope
for the future.
Debbie and James
Maddux

Christmas 2000
Jacob Maddux

Other Books by Lisa Birnbach
1,003 Great Things About Getting Older
The Official Preppy Handbook
Lisa Birnbach College Books
Going to Work
Loose Lips

Other Books by Ann Hodgman
1,003 Great Things About Getting Older
My Baby-sitter Is a Vampire (series)
Stinky Stanley (series)
Beat This!
Beat That!

Other Books by Patricia Marx
1,003 Great Things About Getting Older
How to Regain Your Virginity
You Can Never Go Wrong by Lying
Blockbuster
Now Everybody Really Hates Me
Now I Will Never Leave the Dinner Table
How to Survive Junior High
Meet My Staff

1,003 GREAT THINGS ABOUT KIDS

Lisa Birnbach,
Ann Hodgman,
Patricia Marx

MJF BOOKS
NEW YORK

Published by MJF Books
Fine Communications
Two Lincoln Square
60 West 66th Street
New York, NY 10023

1,003 Great Things About Kids
Library of Congress Catalog Card Number 99-74462
ISBN 1-56731-357-4

Copyright © 1998 by Lisa Birnbach, Ann Hodgman, Patricia Marx.

This edition published by arrangement with Andrews McMeel
Publishing.

All rights reserved. No part of this publication may be reproduced or
transmitted in any form or by any means, electronic or mechanical,
including photocopy, recording, or any information storage and
retrieval system, without the prior written permission of the
publisher.

Manufactured in the United States of America on acid-free paper

MJF Books and the MJF colophon are trademarks of Fine Creative
Media, Inc.

10   9   8   7   6   5   4   3   2   1

1,003 GREAT THINGS ABOUT KIDS

You can make
a toddler laugh uproariously
by simply
sticking out your tongue.

◆

They don't need makeup.

Don't they
look just darling
on Christmas cards?

✦

Eventually,
they'll leave your house and you get to
keep their built-in bookcases.

✦

For a small raise in allowance,
you can get your child
to perform any household chore.

Toddlers kiss on command.

✦

Babies really do have
"baby-soft" skin.

✦

An excuse
to leave boring parties.

✦

Daughter's off to school?
Read her diary.

*A children's sandbox
makes a handy litterbox for the
next-door neighbor's cats.*

✦

Photogenic without a
hairdresser
or makeup artist!

✦

*Young children make sure
you don't sleep away
the whole morning.*

They can carry their weight
in backpacks.

✦

*They leave the best part
of the lobster on the plate.*

✦

Babies are supposed to be fat.

✦

*Etch-A-Sketch
is actually fun to play with.*

Go ahead!
Turn the clock forward an hour
and call it bedtime.

✦

*They think it's hysterical
if you can work the
word* duty *into a sentence.*

✦

Who else stops crying when you
stick a pacifier in his mouth?

They believe you can beat up their friend's fathers.

✦

You get credit
as a parent
when your
infant learns to wave bye-bye.

✦

*You can beat them
mercilessly at chess.*

A reason to buy cute clothes—
in a small size!
—without having to try them on.

✦

*Fodder for
cocktail-party conversation.*

✦

Someone to install your software.

✦

*They know all the words to
"The Hokey Pokey."*

They can recite the TV schedule.

✦

Babies don't fear commitment.

✦

They do
a much cuter rendition
of the Pledge of Allegiance
than you do.

✦

*Nobody sits near you when you take a
baby on a train.*

Giving your kids names
they'll hate, too.

✦

Nobody loves
your grilled-cheese sandwiches
more than
your own children do.

✦

Easily amused
by a big purple
dinosaur.

You'd look like a pervert
if you went to see
George of the Jungle
alone.

✦

*Someone to hold your hand
on command.*

✦

Until age four,
a child would rather have a nickel
than a dime.

Give them a treat
and serve pizza
. . . night after night after night.

◆

A great audience
for knock-knock jokes.

◆

They know better than you
what's recyclable
and what isn't.

Freckles are
marks of cuteness on kids,
not pre-malignancies.

✦

Give a boy a bar mitzvah
and he'll be busy
writing thank-you notes for life.

✦

With small children by your side,
you can board airplanes first.

*Going to the playground on a
beautiful day
(when nobody ends up
getting stitches in
the emergency room).*

✦

One thing
they'll never ask you for:
a dinette set.

✦

*You can make them
apologize to you.*

She has your dimples.

✦

Breakfast in bed on Mother's Day.

✦

You'll get to relearn
the multiplication tables.

✦

*You can pick up
interesting outside conversations
on the baby monitor.*

You have a good reason
why you can't speak
intelligible English.

◆

An opportunity to read
Charlotte's Web, Treasure Island,
and all those other books
you never read
when you were a kid.

◆

Kids really make you appreciate a
good night's sleep.

GREAT MILESTONES

Day 0:
Nobody you love so much
has ever caused you
such excruciating
physical pain.

1 day:
Your friends can't tell
your newborn
from the others in the nursery,
but she is the most beautiful,
anyway.

1 week:
They say it's just gas at this age,
but his is a real smile.

✦

2 months:
Sleeps through the night.
Bye-bye infomercials.

✦

6 months:
Solid food means
that soon
you can start feeding him leftovers.

✦

8 months:
It sounds like "Goo-goo,"
but *you* know
she is saying,
"I think the universe
is steadily expanding."

10 months:
It's a miracle!
He can't talk yet,
but he designs his first web site.

◆

12 months:
Weight has tripled in one year—
last year that this is a good thing.

◆

18 months:
He stops using a pacifier.
You start using one
to alleviate your anxiety
about his anxiety.

◆

23 months:
The last time her age
can be expressed in months.

2 years:
The Terrible Twos
marks the beginning
of the
twenty-eight-year-long
Age of Rebellion

◆

3 years:
Preschool
twice a week
for an hour and a half.
At last
you can go shopping!

◆

4 years:
Starts to want toys
that you also want.

5 years:
The thrill
of hearing your child
read by himself
for the first time.

✦

6 years:
The thrill of
getting to read
your own book
to yourself
while your child
reads her own book
to herself.

✦

7 years:
Your child
learns the meaning of capitalism
by negotiating
with the tooth fairy.

8 years:
Your child's homework
is now
above your intellectual capabilities.

◆

9 years:
Able to baby-sit
for her younger siblings.
Your disposable yearly income
increases by
several thousand dollars.

◆

10 years:
The first mid-school crisis.

◆

11 years:
Let the body piercing begin!

12 years:
Onset of puberty.
Now your child
can give *you* advice
about sex.

◆

13 years:
Considered a man/woman
by Jewish law,
but you must still give
him/her an allowance.

◆

14 years:
Your daughter
reaches the golden age
to get anorexia and be
thin, thin, thin!

15 years:
Your child comes out of the bathroom
for the first time in six months.
Then goes back in.

✦

16 years:
You have lost a child
but gained a chauffeur.

✦

17 years:
His first fake ID.
Now he doesn't have to stay home
to get drunk.

✦

18 years:
Off to college.
Nobody you love so much
has ever caused you
such excruciating emotional pain.

*A second chance
to get an A
on that science project.*

✦

Easy to tell secrets
around those who don't spell.

✦

*Kids are so time-consuming
you have no time left to worry about
your own life.*

How else are you
going to see
The Nutcracker
every Christmas?

◆

*You can always say
that Jimmy erased all the messages
on the machine.*

◆

The leftover food
on your kid's plate has no calories.

The ballet recital
is a great place to meet
other divorced parents.

✦

They go to sleep
on long car rides
. . . sometimes.

✦

Kids bring down the house
when they speak
at funerals.

Tax breaks for each child.

✦

They're not a drain on the
Social Security system.

✦

Babies give baldness
a good name.

✦

Their plays are shorter
than Broadway plays. And free!

Lugging a four-year-old
all day
is excellent
for upper-body strength.

◆

*There's no reason
an adult can't play
with a yo-yo.*

◆

Slinky toys
relieve stress.

Have you ever met
a baby
who didn't have a cute nose?

◆

Why you *have* to buy
a video camera.

◆

Easier to train a child
than a dog
to retrieve your glasses.

Once you have kids,
you start to understand
why your parents were so strict.

✦

Someone to whom
you can give
Aunt Margie's
rhinestone ring.

✦

They eat free at the hotel buffet!

Toddlers would be lost
without you,
especially in supermarkets.

✦

They never complain
about getting older.

✦

They never make a scene
by sending food back
in restaurants.

They leave no perspiration stains.

✦

The PTA is a hotbed of gossip.

✦

If you like being asked riddles,
get ready for a great time!

✦

*They like to sleep over
at their friends' houses.*

They enjoy
retrieving the golf balls
Daddy hits all over the yard.

✦

They'll see you faster
in the emergency room
if you have a kid with you.

✦

Until age eight,
a kid feels privileged
to be the ball boy/girl
when you play tennis.

No cholesterol problems.

✦

Kids can be *natural* blonds.

✦

Kids don't keep calendars.

✦

Your kid's overbite
enables you
to underwrite
your orthodontist's
trip to Europe.

35

Admit it!
You loved making
that papier-mâché volcano
with baking-soda lava.

◆

You develop a knack
for thinking about other things
while you're reading
their favorite books
for the millionth time.
Yet you
still have *plenty* of exPRESSion in
your voice!

Your *two-year-old*
is a genius.

✦

All toddlers
are geniuses
when it comes
to figuring out
the TV remote.

✦

A lollipop
can last the whole day.

While you are looking
for the missing piece
of your son's
jigsaw puzzle,
you may find
the earring
you lost last year.

◆

Three-year-olds
don't know
if you skip
the wordy parts of
Fluffy Gets a New Hat.

Name your son after Uncle Alden
and improve your chances
of ending up in his will.

✦

They give you something
to brag about
at your college reunion.
Well, talk about anyway.

✦

Photographs of your children
show off your
lovely picture frames.

*So few of their clothes
need to be dry-cleaned.*

✦

Newborns
look fabulous in pastel.

✦

*Without kids,
you'd have to
bring your terrier to
Take Our Daughters
to Work Day.*

WHAT TO SAY TO BRAND-NEW PARENTS

"I know this is the kind of thing
everyone says,
but that really is
the most beautiful baby
I've ever seen."

"I think those eyes
are going to stay blue."

"What are you talking about?
She has lots of hair!"

◆

"Don't worry.
I hear they never give 10's
on the APGARS at this hospital."

◆

"Boy,
you just look into those eyes
and wonder
what they're thinking about,
don't you?"

◆

"Wow, great reflexes!"

◆

"So alert!"

"What a gorgeous head!
His head is hardly mashed!"

◆

"*That* is a baby!"

◆

"Only three weeks old?
He looks
like a seven-week-old!"

◆

"Ten fingers and ten toes, I see."

◆

"I swear he knows your voice."

◆

"She looks exactly like you."

"It's amazing.
He looks
exactly like *both* of you!"

◆

"Count on me to baby-sit!"

◆

"Look, she's holding on
to my finger already!

◆

What a smart baby."

◆

"You always forget
how small they are
at first."

44

"Can you believe
that was inside you?!"

✦

"Did I miss the cigars?"

✦

"Now
that is the grip of a
Hank Aaron."

✦

"This is the best month
to have a newborn
because you can
take him outside."
or
"You don't want
to go outside
in the beginning,
anyway."

"Are his eyes
supposed to roll up
in his head like that?"

◆

"I'm *sure*
they didn't switch her
with another baby
at the hospital."

◆

"I read a study
that said
most high achievers
were colicky babies."

◆

"So,
you going to keep her?"

They'll never
order caviar.

✦

*Nursing
is a good excuse
to show off your
breasts.*

✦

They keep the
battery industry alive.

Sit at a desk
in your daughter's
second-grade class
and feel tall.

✦

You don't
have to go through
a secretary
to get them
on the phone.

✦

They don't have lawyers.

Lisps only make
them cuter . . .
until age five.

✦

Once in a while,
the macaroni necklace
your daughter makes
actually looks nice.

✦

For a while,
they think
liquor tastes like medicine.

They're fearless on a ski slope.

✦

Their bones heal faster than ours.

✦

If they owned keys,
they would never forget
where they put them.

✦

Cowlicks.

They photograph well.

✦

Not afraid
to buck convention
and wear a
Batman costume
to church.

✦

*They think
shoveling snow is fun.*

You can find
a tooth fairy
who works for less
than minimum wage.

✦

Think of zwieback
as biscotti by a different name.

✦

It will never occur to them
that they could refuse
to sit in
the time-out chair.

*You can fit a lot of them
in the backseat of a car
if you must.*

✦

Every so often,
the parents
of your kid's friends
are worth knowing.

✦

*People assume
you are responsible
if you have children.*

When they eat
a lot of salt,
they don't get bloated.

✦

Very few children
have a fear of flying.

✦

Need
a musical instrument?
Try a rattle.

They love
talking on the phone,
even when there's
no one on the other end.

✦

Children
are the only known creatures
who can amuse themselves
all day trying
to dig a hole in the sand
in hopes of reaching China.

*Pediatric dentists
have better videos in their office
than the dentist you go to.*

✦

They provide you
with endless opportunities
for acting like a martyr.

✦

*They can answer
every single question
about skateboarding
in the crossword puzzle.*

They travel
at a vastly reduced rate
on airplanes.

◆

*An excuse to keep
Teddy Grahams, Pop-Tarts,
and M&M's
in the house.*

◆

At last,
someone you can beat
in a race or spelling bee.

You can ground them.

✦

They make Christmas bearable.

✦

Toddlers
can learn a language
much faster than you,
no matter how many
Berlitz courses you take.

They can't tell
the difference between
antiques
and reproductions.

✦

*If you start
early enough, you can
serve them
bottles straight
from the refrigerator.*

If you're
unlucky enough
to have to keep
the class guinea pig
over vacation,
at least your kids
will stop wanting
their own guinea pig.

✦

You can give
your teenagers books
that you want
to read yourself.

For some reason,
people think it's a big honor
when you ask them
to be a godparent.

✦

It's true!
When they imitate you, it is the
most sincere form of flattery.

✦

Milk and cookies
is so much safer
than happy hour.

They'll never know
if you eat
a few of the
Gummi Bears.

✦

Look cute in clothes
that don't fit.

✦

Monkey-like
climbing skills.

SIMPLE PLEASURES

Pushing the button in the elevator

✦

Turning a light switch on and off

✦

Throwing coins in the tollbooth basket

✦

Standing on Daddy's feet to waltz

63

Taking everything out of Mommy's purse

✦

Looking through Daddy's wallet

✦

Staying up a half an hour later

✦

Walking up the slide

✦

Licking the batter out of the bowl

✦

Putting lightning bugs in a jar

Sitting on your lap

✦

Sitting in the front seat

✦

Getting the window seat on the train

✦

Party shoes

✦

Watching a sibling being punished

✦

A grown-up jangling keys

Helping you with anything

✦

Wearing *your* shoes

✦

Jumping on the bed

✦

Anything forbidden

✦

Anything chocolate

✦

Trucks

A dollar

✦

Snow

✦

Ice cubes

✦

Playing with pots and pans

✦

Stacking cans of cat food

✦

Pulling all the books out of the bookcase

Bubble wrap

✦

Sparklers

✦

Burping

✦

The chicken wishbone

✦

Shells

✦

Worms

At last,

you really *can't* find the time

to exercise.

◆

They owe you

their lives.

And you can make sure

they never forget that.

◆

They don't hold a grudge

. . . for long.

Enviable metabolism.

✦

Children believe you
when you say
that the local toy store
no longer sells Barbies.

✦

Watching your son
jump off the diving board means
so much to him.

You can buy designer
night-lights.

✦

The age of a young child
tends to be given
in terms of months,
which sharpens
your mathematical skills.

✦

Babies get whatever they want
without talking.

They can make a ton of money
doing commercials.

◆

Kids pull off
the missing-front-tooth
look much better
than adults.

◆

Your baby will never know
if you exchange
the baby-shower presents
for something you really want.

A Portacrib is a good place
for a puppy, too.

✦

When your child wakes up
with a nightmare,
you can practice your
dream analysis technique.

✦

Until she's five,
your daughter
will believe you when you tell her
Chap Stick is lipstick.

Digital clocks
make it easier for kids
to tell you what time it is.

✦

Their knees don't crack.

✦

So what if baby teeth develop cavities.

✦

Unlike you,
small children actually like being
tossed in a blanket.

*The average IQ rises with
every new generation.
Why, soon a toddler will be able to
outsmart Stephen Hawkings.*

✦

They like chocolate pudding better
than chocolate mousse.

✦

*They like
ready-made pudding better
than the stuff you make
from the package.*

No bunions.

✦

Adults without children
look funny
ordering hot cocoa.

✦

Children don't need root canal.

✦

Plenty of Cliffs Notes
lying around the house.

They think
Jell-O is a treat.

✦

To a baby,
being held upside down
is like a ride
in a twin-engine plane.

✦

They like
cheap wrapping paper
better than expensive.

*They don't
fuss about
being rained on.*

✦

To a child,
adding food coloring
counts as a recipe.

✦

*Silly Putty
isn't so silly.*

You are less likely
to have houseguests
if you station
baby gates everywhere.

✦

The older ones stay in school
all day long.

✦

Painting by numbers
is surprisingly rewarding.

Living with a teenager
means you're up on all the slang.

✦

You get very, very good
at going back to projects
you were interrupted
in the middle of.

✦

You get
a thorough grounding in all the words
to all the
Raffi songs ever written.

Teens with driver's licenses
love being asked
to run errands.

✦

Night feedings:
a good way to catch up
on late-night public-access TV.

✦

Finally,
a chance to relearn
(or learn!)
all the state capitals.

Making a candle stay upright
in a pumpkin
improves wrist dexterity.

✦

If you're sentimental,
you now have many more
opportunities to cry.

✦

Formula stains
give you the excuse
to try many, many different kinds
of detergent.

Little League practices
are an excellent way
to release your own aggression.

✦

*All that carpooling
has really helped you learn
about your community.*

✦

When you chaperone
on a field trip,
you get to see how much worse
everyone else's kids behave
than yours.

THE COST
OF A BABY
VERSUS
THE COST OF YOU

Pampers:	$8.00 *a box*
La Perla panties	$120.00 *a pair*

pacifier	$2.75

(lasts a week, or until child drops it out of the stroller somewhere in Central Park)

Prozac	$42.00

(for a week's supply)

tube of Desitin	$3.00
tube of Renova	$75.00

haircut with lollipop	$10.00
styling and highlights	$85.00

play group	FREE
(but you have to serve refreshments)	
group therapy	$100.00
	(a session)

onesie	$5.95
Donna Karan body suit	$195.00

Cozy Coupe	$250.00
Jeep Cherokee	$30,000.00

Cheerios and a bottle of apple juice	*under* $10.00
dinner with wine	$100.00

no pillow	$0.00
dust-mite-proof pillow	$54.00
crib mobile	$25.00
Calder mobile	$3,000,000.00
stickers	$2.00 *for ten*
tattoos	$150.00 *a piece*
Goodnight Moon	$12.95
Valium	$122.00

Their belief in Santa Claus
can be used to
your advantage.

✦

Baby powder smells great.

✦

They don't have as far to fall.

✦

For the next ten years or so,
you'll get to indulge
your secret lust for fast food.

Working on
your child's diorama
is a lot more fun for you
than it is
for your child.

✦

The more houses
you allow your kids
to trick-or-treat at,
the better the selection of candy
you'll be able
to steal from their stash
later on.

Save money
on Christmas presents
for your baby!
She isn't old enough to care.

✦

The shallow end of the pool
is warmer
than the deep end.

✦

To your child,
you're an expert
at practically everything.

Breast-feeding
gives you the perfect excuse
to stay home.

✦

*Some of those
Gerber baby desserts
are actually pretty good.*

✦

Come on.
Haven't you always *wanted*
a minivan?

Come on.
Haven't you always wanted
a puppy?

✦

Come on.
Haven't you always *wanted*
to go to Busch Gardens?

✦

Theirs is the only hair
that really looks good
in plastic barrettes.

You really, really know
how to clean off
a high-chair tray.

✦

*You get
pllllllenty of practice
letting down hems.*

✦

There's no law against
a parent using children's Tylenol.

Giving them presents
is better than receiving
the presents they make you
in nursery school.

✦

If you're towing a small child,
people will sometimes
let you have their seat
on the bus—
not always,
but sometimes.

Finally, a reason to buy
The Wizard of Oz,
How the Grinch Stole Christmas,
and all the other kids videos
you secretly love.

✦

You get a lot of mileage out of
a tiny box of raisins.

✦

Parents get to make
other people's kids
say please and thank you.

Pretty soon
your kids will be old enough
for summer camp.

✦

*You can order Venus flytraps
from catalogs.*

✦

Telling your children
stories about things you did as a kid
is more entertaining
(to them, at least)
than you'd possibly believe.

You don't have to
knock yourself out
providing homemade cookies.

✦

*Whether your child
goes to public or private school,
you can always feel smug
about the choice you made.*

✦

You can't get
into some children's museums
without a child.

*They might ask
for sips of your Coke,
but they won't ask
for sips of your beer.*

◆

Pampers are great
for plugging up leaks
in the ceiling.

◆

*They never notice
when you flush their guppies
down the toilet.*

Their school band concerts
generally end by
9:00 A.M.

✦

Backpacking babies
gives you
good shoulder muscles.

✦

To a kid,
an old joke
seems brand-new.

*If you run out of
deodorant, shampoo,
or razor blades,
you* know
your teen's got some.

◆

A puddle on the driveway
is entertainment.

◆

*You can force a toddler
to dress the way
you want him to.*

Kids actually *like*
to hear you sing.

✦

Even for parents,
snow days are fun…
for the first hour
or so.

✦

Subscribe to *Highlights*
and catch up on
Goofus and Gallant's escapades!

Children delight
in recording the message
on the family phone machine.
(And how much more fetching
than your
monotonous voice!)

◆

Once you have kids,
your own mother
is suddenly
a lot more useful.

THE BEST THING ABOUT BEING A KID

"You can't go to jail."
—*Hunter Stuart, age fourteen*

◆

"You have somebody
to set the table for you."
—*John Owen, age ten*

◆

"Recess."
—*Kyle Morton, age nine*

"You get to stand up on a chair
when you sing the Shabbat song."
—*Greta Kline, age four*

◆

"If you're too tired to walk,
someone carries you.
But now I'm old."
—*Rachel Marx, age four*

◆

"When your parents
spell p-r-e-s-e-n-t,
you know
they're getting you something."
—*Sam Haft, age seven*

◆

"Piggybacks
my dad gives me."
—*Avalon Nicholas Wolf, age five*

"You don't have to work out."
—*Elizabeth Buckley*
Harrold O'Donnell, age three

✦

"Allowance."
—*Peter Walters, age nine*

✦

"You don't have to
pay taxes."
—*Charles Winkoff, age eight*

✦

"No bills."
—*Alan Hyer, age seven*

✦

"Picking your nose."
—*Eric Dominick, age nine*

"You don't have to
change diapers."
—*Cynthia Speer, age nine*

✦

"You get allowance
just for cleaning your room."
—*Katie Toplyn, age seven*

✦

"In play school,
you *have* to play and stuff."
—*Boco Haft, age four*

✦

"You can
drive your parents crazy."
—*"Cous-cous" Chamoux, age eight*

"You don't have to
stay at work late."
—*Adam Ross, age six*

◆

"Your parents buy you stuff."
—*Henry Dwyer, age eight*

◆

"Kids' birthday parties are better
than grown-ups' birthday parties."
—*Helen Ribicoff, age seven*

◆

"Moms borrow your money
and give you a couple dollars more.
My mom owes me twenty dollars."
—*Beatrice Lacy, age eight*

"You have more time
to play handball."
—*Michael Siracuse, age eight*

◆

"You don't have
brittle bones."
—*Claire Morley, age eleven*

◆

"You don't have to
read the newspaper
while sitting on the toilet."
—*Benjamin Chase, age eight*

◆

"You don't have to
support a family."
—*Rose Pierpont, age ten*

"You don't have to
worry about your boss firing you.
Plus, kids get to meet new people
which adults don't have
the opportunity to do
because they're always
on the train
or talking to people they already know."
—*Allie Borowitz, age eight*

✦

"You get goodie bags
at birthday parties."
—*Michael Birnbach, age eight*

✦

"When you're a kid,
you don't have to
rush everywhere."
—*Bennett See, age nine*

"My grandpa
has no teeth.
The good thing
about being a kid
is you have teeth."
—*Harry Mathew Geller, age seven*

✦

"Say you're in Connecticut
and your little brother
is sitting in the swing
and talking to himself.
It looks kind of cute,
but
if you're a grown-up
and you talk to yourself,
it looks weird."
—*Alexander Warner, age eight*

Collages: children's folk art.

✦

*Putting a carrot
in a glass of water
counts as gardening.*

✦

Spitting on a Kleenex
counts as washing a kid's face.

✦

*An apple slice
counts as a vegetable.*

A grocery-store receipt
counts as stationery
for a teacher's note.

✦

You have a new appreciation
of bulldozers, fire engines,
and other large machines.

✦

For a kid,
taking the car through the car wash
is almost as good
as a movie.

*Pretty soon
you'll be able to borrow
your daughter's clothes.*

✦

Without kids,
there'd be no point
to April Fool's.

✦

*Kids provide
a good reason
to start going
to church again.*

Their baths
kill a good hour
before bedtime.

◆

*For several years,
you'll at least be able
to get stuff done
during their naps.*

◆

Johnson's baby shampoo
really *doesn't* sting.

What looks like
a noisy construction site to you
is a living art gallery to them.

✦

It takes a while
before they notice that paste,
which is washable, isn't as good
as glue, which isn't.

✦

Since little kids look so adorable
without a waist,
maybe you do, too.

Little girls keep the vast
party-dress-smocking industry
alive.

◆

*Don't you love
that childlike sense of wonder
about potty jokes?*

◆

Fighting with your teenager
about her hair
keeps you from fighting
about worse things.

To an infant,
you are God.

✦

Cleaning up throw-up
keeps you humble.

✦

Scientific advances
in instant-read thermometers
benefit
the entire population.

It's really easy
to scare kids,
if you're so inclined.

✦

Marshmallows
are acceptable as a dessert.

✦

Dazzle your offspring with
your "clairvoyance" in
I Love Lucy episodes.

Children
are the best possible excuse
for quitting smoking.

✦

They think it's fun
to hail a cab.

✦

You can hide
their most odious toys,
and they'll
forget about them.

Most boys don't care
if all their toy soldiers
are built to the same scale.

◆

*Going to Disney World
is more fun
than going to a resort.*

◆

You can save money
on shoes
until they can actually walk.

Buying a new box of crayons
is always a thrill—
for you and them.

◆

They prefer
cheap plastic sleds
to expensive wooden ones.

◆

There is endless comic potential
in a toddler
wearing Daddy's shoes.

You wouldn't want
a grown-up flower girl
at your wedding,
would you?

✦

For a preschooler,
taking a walk
to the drugstore
to buy a Popsicle
can easily become
a full-day activity.

They never become
blasé about getting mail.

✦

*Any restaurant
with a tablecloth
counts as fine dining.*

✦

Seeing all those
Salvation Army Santa Clauses
gives you lots of chances
to perfect your Santa explanation.

*They can't tell
the difference
between
butter and margarine.*

✦

If you
have to move
to a foreign country,
your kids
will soon be able
to interpret for you.

No matter
how much they cry
when they have a baby-sitter,
you'll *forget all about it*
by the time
you've pulled out of
the driveway.

✦

Global warming
means less time spent
wrestling babies
into their snowsuits.

TOTALLY ARBITRARY RULES YOUR KIDS (PROBABLY) WON'T QUESTION

If you spill your milk
one more time,
this meal is over.

◆

Don't call your mother *she*.

You have to eat
six bites of chicken.
Well, three bites.

No one touches
Grandma's crystal bowls
in the living room
unless an adult is present.

Don't read the Sunday comics out loud.

✦

Before you go to sleep,
it's okay to read in bed
for half an hour,
but not to play
quietly in your room
for half an hour.

In this family,
we do not imitate Big Bird.

✦

Five library books—that's the limit.

✦

You can jump
from the fifth step.
The sixth step is too high.

✦

You can't have
your ears pierced
until you're
nine . . . seven . . . five . . .
until some girl in your class
whose mother is
kind of like me
lets her get hers pierced.

You can put
ketchup on your fries,
but not on your potato chips.

◆

You can keep
caterpillars in a jar,
but not slugs.

◆

No matter
how much you hate it,
you have to take
piano for two years
—just to see if you like it.

◆

No humming when
Mommy is trying
to parallel-park.

You can open only
two Christmas presents
before breakfast.

✦

You can put your elbows
on the table
and chew with your mouth open
only when you have a friend
over for supper.

✦

You can play with your toy cars
at the table
as long as
you don't put them
on your plate.

✦

That room
is for grown-ups only.

They admire you
for drinking scary things
like coffee and beer.

✦

Baby teeth
are infinitely more attractive
than permanent ones.

✦

You can cut
a baby's nails
without waking her up.

They never
seem to get sick
of chicken noodle soup,
do they?

◆

For several years,
you can trick them
into thinking that
FAO Schwarz
is a museum rather
than a place
to spend money.

*Hearing about the class bully
makes you really, really glad
you're old.*

✦

It could be worse.
You could be
home-schooling them.

✦

*They really will thank you
for those music lessons
someday.*

If you cut
an apple in half crosswise,
you'll see a star.

✦

You learn a lot
about responsibility
when you
take care
of the pets
your kids
don't take care of.

Children
are the only people
who look nice in
heart-shaped sunglasses.

✦

*You get so you can
feed and change
an infant at two A.M.
without even
opening your eyes.*

✦

A reason to go on a water slide.

Chances are good
that your baby
will sleep through the night
at some point.

✦

Children think
dandelions are pretty.

✦

You can usually
blow some really good bubbles
before the jar
of bubble stuff spills.

Head lice
are a good way to learn
about survival of the fittest.

✦

*A sweet potato plant
on Father's Day.*

✦

Plastic place mats
are easier to clean
than the grown-up kind.

Old cloth diapers
make the best dust cloths.

✦

Sturdy,
scaled-down furniture
makes a good footstool
for an adult.

✦

Baby wipes are good
for cleaning spots
off rugs.

Babies don't complain
when you coat
their chapped cheeks
with Vaseline.

✦

Those
handprint-in-clay paperweights
make good presents
for grandparents—
year after year
after year after year.

They think
Bil Keane's *Family Circus*
is funny.

✦

In summertime,
they get so dirty
that it's a genuine pleasure
to give them a bath.

✦

Warner Brothers
has some good programs.

Easily embarrassed teens
are more *than willing*
to help moms keep
their wardrobes up to date.

✦

As long as you're paying
for their haircuts,
you get to tell
the stylist what to do.

✦

As long as you're paying for
their clothes, you get final say.

Kids don't mind
wearing mismatched socks
as much
as you'd think.

✦

They teach you
a new appreciation
for the lowest forms of life,
like worms
and caterpillars.

You can go
either way
when they step
on ants.
Either it's
a harmless pastime
or it's a good chance
to teach morals.

✦

They are
physically incapable
of having sex
for several years.

If they misbehave
in church,
everyone has to be
nice about it.

◆

*They think mutts
are just as good as
pedigreed dogs.*

◆

They never seem to care
when their teddy bear
loses an eye.

You can get them
to address
your Christmas cards.

✦

Until age six,
they think hand-me-downs
are a privilege.

✦

They're easier to distract
than dogs and cats.

GREAT EUPHEMISMS FOR BRAT

Spunky

✦

Feisty

✦

Determined

✦

High-spirited

Going through a growth spurt

✦

Going through a phase

✦

High-strung

✦

High-energy

✦

Chatterbox

✦

Bouncing off the walls

✦

All boy

Daddy's girl

✦

Knows his/her own mind

✦

Independent

✦

A little clingy today

✦

Coming down with something

✦

Having a bad day

✦

Rambunctious

Precocious

◆

Tired

◆

Ready for a nap

◆

Just getting ready
to stop taking naps

Fussy

◆

Colicky

Coming down
with another ear infection

◆

Must be teething

◆

Two years old

◆

Preteen

◆

Adolescent

In a world without children,
the works of Beatrix Potter
would never have come to light.

✦

You can make a
quick, inexpensive change
to their bedrooms
merely by adding
a wallpaper border.

✦

Foreign children speak their native
languages with uncanny skill.

They like
pressing down on the string
so you can make
a knot on a package.

◆

They never notice the difference
between pancakes
made from scratch
and pancakes made from a mix.

◆

They'll grow up
and cook Thanksgiving dinner.

You're less likely
to go to the trouble
and expense of
building a swimming pool
in your backyard
when you have children—
pools are so dangerous!

✦

When your children
aren't in the car,
you can strap bags
of fragile groceries
into the car seat.

Imagine!
Even a tiny, tiny newborn
has her own fingerprints!

✦

In a restaurant,
a kid is a cheap date.

✦

At last!
Zip-up neckties
for preschool boys.

Their innate bad taste
makes them far less critical
of gaudiness and vulgarity
than you are.

✦

In a strange situation, you can fool
children into thinking you're not
scared because you're a grown-up.

✦

They're not ashamed
to order sprinkles
on their ice-cream cones.

They almost never
need bifocals.

◆

*Hair stylists
don't usually mind
when you have to
bring your baby
to your appointment.*

◆

You can get them
to pass hors d'oeuvres
when you have parties.

Those little plastic wading pools
are a great place
to give your houseplants
a soaking.

◆

You can finish
their hamburger, too—
they had only one bite.

◆

They don't need
to wash their hair very often.

You can finish their soda
when they get a hamburger at
McDonald's.

✦

*You can eat their pickle
when they order a hamburger at
McDonald's.*

✦

You can sneak some of their fries
when they order a hamburger at
McDonald's.

Save money on the circus—
most kids
are afraid of clowns.

✦

Infants burp
so astonishingly loudly
you sort of look *forward*
to burping them.

✦

Pediatricians
don't give out lollipops anymore,
but they do give out stickers.

Refrigerator art.

◆

*Their first somersault is always
such an accomplishment!*

◆

When kids are around, you tend
to go on picnics more often.

◆

*They look so funny chasing their tails—
oh, no, wait a minute,
that's puppies.*

As soon as they realize that
"We'll see" means no,
you can go back to having it mean
"We'll see."

✦

You can instantly
shut a kid up by just turning
on the TV.

✦

Anything you hide on a high shelf
doesn't exist for a kid
under four feet tall.

They don't get lower back pain.

✦

They admire
your rock-skipping ability.

✦

They're braver
about swimming in cold water
than you.

✦

A double chin is attractive
when you're under five.

*A newborn's soft spot
is endlessly fascinating
to older siblings.*

✦

They're *more* than happy
to decorate all the cakes
you ever feel like baking.

✦

*You have an excuse
to get a subscription to*
Mad *magazine.*

All that money
you spent on educating them:
at least you won't be losing it
on the slot machines.

◆

If your teenager
gets a tattoo,
at least you have the comfort
of knowing that it will
really, really hurt
when he finally decides
to get it removed.

They think
the teacher is
granting them
a special favor
when she lets them erase
the chalkboard.

✦

Admit it:
you've always wanted
to get some
baby shoes bronzed.

If they plant a garden,
they'll forget about it
before they realize
nothing's ever going to come up.

✦

Mrs. Piggle-Wiggle
is one of the best characters in fiction.

✦

Beeswax is much less messy
than Play-Doh,
and it never dries out.

IT'S EASIER
THAN EVER
TO RAISE A KID
TODAY

Parades now televised,
allowing you
to get a better view
than if you were
actually there

✦

Mini-juice containers
with their own straws

No drummer boys
in modern armies

✦

Saturday-morning TV
every morning,
thanks to the miracle
of taping

✦

Every kid
with his own
entertainment system
in the car,
thanks to the
Walkman

Entire books full of
science fair projects

Diapers with Velcro

The Disney Store

Children's museums

Unspillable sippy-cups

Ultra-flexible
indestructible eyeglasses

Polar fleece baby bags

✦

Flip-top
bubble-gum-flavored
toothpaste

✦

Sunblock

✦

Books on tape

✦

Catalog shopping

✦

Colored braces
for your kids' teeth

Instant-read thermometers

✦

Better designed
infant seats

✦

Organic baby food
(if you care)

✦

Simpler tax regulations
for foreign nannies

✦

Beepers and cell phones

All kids prefer store-bought treats—
Dunkin' Munchkins,
Carvel cakes, Snickers bars—
to homemade ones.

◆

We can all learn a lot
from a child's laissez-faire attitude
about cleaning up her room.

◆

They don't mind
if you get lost in the car;
they love it!

When they can't think
of anything to do,
they (sometimes)
like polishing your silver.

✦

If you don't tell them
it's possible,
they'll never expect
to use
fingerpaints at home.

If you don't tell them
it's possible,
they'll never expect
to arrive
at birthday parties
on time.

◆

If you don't tell them
it's possible,
they'll never expect
to eat in the living room.

Even adolescents thrill
to the sight of
Mickey Mouse,
sort of.

✦

*Preschoolers can be conned
into "painting" the house
with water.*

✦

At fairs and carnivals, you can
cram enough food into them
to last the whole day.

They love to make
"difficult" phone calls
for you.

✦

After age ten,
giving them presents
is easy—
all they want is cash.

✦

Flight attendants
give them activity packs.

The ability to turn
a circular driveway
into at least a thousand
different playing fields.

✦

*Why, their pores
are practically invisible!*

✦

Kids display amazing ingenuity
in the matter of customizing
their school uniforms.

*They never care
if their bathing-suit legs
are cut too high.*

✦

They can reach
into small spaces
to get things you've dropped.

✦

*There has never been
a boy who didn't look smart
in a navy blazer.*

Haunted hayrides
really *are* fun
for the whole family.

✦

*Your seven-year-old
can translate your
two-year-old's speech for you.*

✦

They're awfully patient
about constantly being asked the
same questions by adults.

Your son's saxophone
sounds so awful
that you don't
mind the fact
that he practices
for only one minute
a day.

✦

Tubby three-year-old girls
look a lot cuter
in bikinis
than tubby thirty-year-old moms.

Forgot to bring
your sand toys
to the beach?
Don't worry.
Someone else
will have forgotten
to bring theirs home
from *the beach.*

◆

Possibly your winning ticket to
America's Funniest Home Videos.

*It's amazing
how many of them
already know the
Heimlich maneuver.*

✦

Just when you think
you've forgotten
how to play crazy eights,
your kids get old enough
to teach it to you
again.

They won't touch
any dessert
that has rum in it,
so there'll be more for you.

◆

It's not
as disastrous socially
when their noses
need blowing.

◆

A leftover stroller
makes a great grocery-hauler.

The mere sight
of a rabbit on the lawn
makes their day.

✦

Babies never accuse you
of getting too personal.

✦

A baby doesn't mind
looking vulnerable.

✦

They're open to bribes.

If you train your kids early,

they need never know

they can order

their ice cream

in a cone

instead of a cup.

✦

Adorable scaled-down Suzuki violins.

✦

When your daughter outgrows

her dollhouse, you can have it.

Although children
do shout too much,
at least it's not because
they're going deaf.

✦

Colic is not your fault.

✦

A dad doing errands
with a baby
gets masses of help
from everyone he encounters.

YOU'LL NEVER RUN OUT OF

Play-Doh

✦

Children's Tylenol

✦

Individually wrapped
cheese slices

✦

Apple juice

Hercules Band-aids

✦

Crayons on the rug

✦

Mysterious objects
behind the sofa cushions

✦

Pipe cleaners

✦

Dirty walls

✦

Magnetic letters
for the refrigerator door

Lego bricks

✦

Tiny rubber bands for braces

✦

"Extra" puzzle pieces

✦

Name tags
you never got around
to sewing on clothes

✦

Christmas-card photos
you never got around
to mailing

Snapshots
you never got around
to putting in the album

◆

Money-saving coupons
that have expired

◆

Old jars
of spaghetti sauce
with little bits of mold

◆

But you will run out of
Pampers

You'll eventually cave in
on every single one
of your prohibitions
(no TV, no comic books,
no candy, no Sony PlayStation).
Why not give in now
and eliminate
all that tension?

◆

Your old toys
seem like prehistoric wonders
when you take your kids
to your parents' house.

It's just as cute
when a second grader
forgets his lines
in the school play
as when he's word-perfect.
Especially if he's
someone else's
second grader.

`✦

Many elementary-school teachers would
actually prefer
not to get
Christmas presents.

Nobody thinks
you're gay
if you have a kid.

✦

They think we're brilliant.

✦

A bag of in-the-shell walnuts
plus a colander
makes one of the
world's best bath toys.

*Preschoolers don't notice
when their bathwater goes cold;
they just keep playing.*

◆

Little ones
will let you dress them
like Madame Alexander dolls.

◆

*When it's their turn to subtract,
suddenly you feel like a genius.*

They all look good in baseball caps.

✦

You can buy more Barbies.

✦

Not to mention
the Barbie Cool Looks
Fashion Designer CD-ROM.

✦

*Take a child on a hike
and you don't have
to walk fast.*

They don't realize
how dumb hopscotch is.

✦

Baby Gap, Gap Kids,
OshKosh B'Gosh, Gymboree,
Little Me, Baby Dior.

✦

Reading to your kid's class.

✦

Someone to pass
Grandma's recipes to.

You can play Monopoly
on a rainy afternoon.

✦

For a time they believe you
when you tell them,
"Sunday school is fun! *"*
"Hebrew school is fun! *"*
"Math tutoring is fun! *"*
"Piano lessons are fun! *"*

✦

Play your cards right and they'll
send you to a good nursing home.

*They love it
when you wear something
that matches
what they're wearing.*

◆

Beanie Babies *are* kind of cute.

◆

Kids are costume-friendly.

◆

Lots of visits to the
cute pediatrician.

Now you can watch
Sesame Street *with abandon.*

✦

Dr. Seuss is just as great
the second, third, or fourth time
around.

✦

Kids can tell the Olsen twins apart.

✦

They can watch the same video
over and over and over.

Kangarockaroos
are a convenient place
to dump old newspapers.

✦

Forget the cost
of expensive orthodontia:
when you see them
sucking their thumb in bed,
it's too cute for words.

✦

Plenty of opportunities to visit
hands-on exhibits at museums.

Wow!
Your daughter
can have sex with the
president of the United States!

✦

*No one will stop you
when you boast about
your children's accomplishments.*

✦

Kids think that hot dogs
make a gourmet meal.

*Your children actually think
you are stylish.*

✦

You can send them away
for two months
in the summer.

✦

*Even a half-birthday
can be an event . . .
or an excuse for a party.*

In elementary school,
fights get resolved easily.

✦

They will eat
the medicine
you bury in applesauce.

✦

It's okay if they don't
brush their baby teeth:
they fall out,
anyway.

Great messengers
between you
and your spouse.

◆

How proud do you feel
pushing a stroller?

◆

Certain clothes
look really adorable
in small sizes:
leather jackets, clogs,
fringed western jackets.

Your opportunity
to hire nubile foreign au pairs.

✦

*You can tell them
the frozen yogurt
is ice cream
and they'll believe you.*

✦

They're so self-absorbed
that they don't notice
when you zone out of
a conversation.

TOPICS YOU'LL NEVER HAVE TO DISCUSS WITH A KID

The NASDAQ

◆

Directions

◆

The mortgage

205

Chilean fruit-spraying methods

The astonishing success
of new
anti-impotence drugs

Whether it's better
to quick-roast
or slow-roast
a chicken

The decline
of family values

The telecommunications bill

✦

Face-lifts

✦

How much
to tip the waitress

✦

Are the McBeans
getting a divorce?

✦

What kind
of tooth crown to get

What kind
of kitchen counter to get

✦

Price of gasoline

✦

Mommy and Daddy's
sex life

✦

The best place to retire

Sharing your
favorite books with them.

✦

They have a better chance
than you of growing up
and becoming president.

✦

Kids don't notice
when you rehang
the Christmas ornaments
they hung too close together.

Someone to browse the Web for you.

✦

Your wicked brother
can't touch
your child's trust fund.

✦

Someone to call you
Mommy or Daddy.

✦

Cute valentines
to buy for the whole class.

Kids smell great . . .

at least

for the first few years . . .

at least

some of the time.

✦

Maybe

they'll hold on

to their virginity

until they're

. . . fifteen.

It has been calculated
that by the time
babies born in 1998
go to college,
their four years
will cost approximately
$190,000.
But don't despair.
Think of it as a financial goal.

✦

*A reason to carry
a bottle of antibacterial spray
around with you at all times.*

Satisfied by action pictures.

✦

Kids can't give you rabies.

✦

They won't fight you
for the phone
until they're six.

✦

*You can buy cooperation
for the price
of a small ice-cream cone.*

You can buy love.

✦

There's always the chance
that when they grow up,
your children
will like each other.

✦

They don't need
to play golf.
Riding in the cart is enough.

*Whom can you live
vicariously through
if not your children?*

◆

One of your children
might buy you a house
someday.

◆

*They will take care of you
when you're old.*

My daughter,
the Rhodes scholar.

✦

My son,
the indicted congressman.

✦

All our old favorite toys
have been miniaturized
and put on key chains
for our kids.

*Lower rate
of incarceration
than rest
of the population.*

✦

When you're
in a crappy mood,
they are more sensitive to it
than your mate.

They think
you're more beautiful than
Anastasia,
more handsome than
John Smith,
stronger than
Hercules,
and more powerful than
Aladdin's genie.

✦

The only species
that looks good
in a rain hat.

Tiny toes.

◆

Tickling them.

◆

They think
it's grown up
to help carry the groceries.

◆

Matching
Lilly Pulitzer mother-daughter
wardrobes.

*Most girls
prefer costume jewelry
to the real thing.*

✦

Unsolicited signs of affection.

✦

*They're less afraid
of trespassing rodents
than you are;
in fact,
they'd like
to adopt them as pets.*

They know how to be
properly blackmailed.

✦

*Show them cat's cradle
and they think
you're amazing.*

✦

Mr. Rogers is *still* living
in the neighborhood.

✦

Let's face it: pouting is cute.

221

Someone
to enter all those beauty contests
you couldn't enter
because of your
glandular condition.

✦

An excuse to see
The Lion King *on Broadway.*

✦

How would the counter person
ever know
the Happy Meal was really for you?

*The sound
of kids' snoring
isn't unbearable.*

◆

If you order
in French at a restaurant,
it sounds pretentious;
if Junior orders in French,
it sounds . . . *incroyable.*

◆

*Someone to go to the
Spice Girls concert with you.*

KIDS
TEACH YOU TO
THINK FAST

"Why do I have
to take French
when everyone
in France
already speaks English?"

◆

"But how does the seed
get together
with the egg?"

"Why are you
making me
take trumpet
when you *know*
I'll end up quitting?

"Why does God
allow mean people?"

"Where does my mind go
when I'm sleeping?"

"Are Bert and Ernie primates?"

"Then why don't you
send my dinner
to the starving children?"

◆

"Why am I not older?
I've been here
for so many years."

◆

"How does the car work?"

◆

"What color is that lady's hair?"

◆

"If most accidents
happen ten miles
from your house,
why don't we move?"

"How did the witch
get the idea
to do that to
Hansel and Gretel?"

◆

"If you had to pick—
say someone
forced you—
would you pick
Tommy or me?"

◆

"What if
the person driving the car
in back of us
is blind?"

They give you
the opportunity
to use the term *girl*
without being
politically incorrect.

✦

You can try on
your teenage daughter's
Hard Candy nail polish or
platform sandals or
retro hair accessories
while she's at school.

Thank you,
Nickelodeon,
every mommy's helper.

✦

In every issue of
Parents *magazine*
there is at least
one usable child-rearing tip.

✦

God bless that Shari Lewis.

Small children
prefer boxes
to anything
that comes
inside the boxes.

◆

Someone's got to wear
green pearlized nail polish.

◆

Cute misspellings
make a thank-you note
even cuter.

They consider
singing the song
"The Wheels on the Bus"
a whole morning's
entertainment.

◆

Twenty dollars
buys a very generous
birthday present.
Twenty-five dollars
makes you look like
Eugene Lang.

You can give them
trendy, chic names,
unlike, say,
Patty, Ann, or Lisa.

✦

Your daughter's crush on
Noah Wyle
makes yours look healthy.

✦

You can steal
from your kid's collection
of condoms.

*Your kids know
where to buy the best pot.*

✦

You can sneak
into your daughter's room
and stare at her poster
of the current teen hunk.

✦

*Since your kid
belongs to the soccer league,
you are within your rights
looking like a soccer mom.*

Kids' clothes
rarely require ironing.

✦

*You don't have to try hard
when you play hide-and-seek
with a child.*

✦

Paid maternity leave.

✦

*Seeing a choo-choo train
makes their day.*

An excuse
to hang a tire from a tree.

✦

*They think it's fun
when the electricity goes out.*

✦

Kids eat free at
Jimmy's Bait Shack in Manhattan!

✦

*A genuinely talented child actor
is one of life's great miracles.*

You can take off
a couple of hours
from work
for a parent-teacher conference.

✦

Now you have
snapshots to put in your wallet.

✦

For many years,
they have no hang-ups
about nudity.

An acute sense
of hearing.

◆

You can get
a nanny to take care of them
all day long . . .
until the sitter
comes at night.

◆

Use stickers
if you run out of Scotch tape.

With proper delivery,
your puns can make you
the most popular coach
in Little League.

◆

*They're young enough
not to mind the
Joanie and Chachi episodes of*
Happy Days.

◆

They don't care
how ugly their shoes are,
as long as they're platforms.

It's almost inspiring,
the number of ways
they can come up with
to stay up later.

◆

Virtual pets
are less work for mothers
than real pets.

◆

Young enough to love—
really, really love—
Leonardo DiCaprio.

And to maybe
have a chance with him.

✦

*You can pick
your child's friends.*

✦

Under the age of thirteen,
the human body
is actually 36 percent
Chicken McNuggets.

No unsightly body hair.

✦

Bad breath
begins in adulthood.

✦

Harmless obsessive crushes.

✦

Claiming your child is sick
gets you out of
any social obligation.

All a newborn
has to do
to be considered alert
is blink.

✦

A balanced meal
is made up of
french fries and ketchup
(starch and vegetable).
Add coffee and milk
and you have dairy, too.

WORLD'S GREATEST PLAY DOUGH RECIPE

2 cups all-purpose flour
½ cup salt
4 teaspoons cream of tartar
2 cups water
2 tablespoons corn oil
Optional food coloring

Mix all the ingredients except the food coloring in a large skillet. Cook and stir over low heat until the mixture thickens and the bottom is just starting to crust up—about 15 minutes. The dough will be very thick and hard to stir at this point.

Turn the dough out onto a large cookie sheet and let it cool. When cool, knead it until smooth; then knead in the optional food coloring. Store in a covered container.

Makes 3 cups.

Collect all twelve
Pizza Hut NBA Souvenir Cups!

✦

They're satisfied with
fairly rudimentary sand castles.

✦

Carrying their bulky luggage
keeps strangers
many feet away from you.

✦

They liven up a divorce case.

Babies don't mind
when sand gets in their food.

✦

At restaurants, they always think
the bread basket is a treat.

✦

They don't learn
how to fake a fever
until they're twelve or so.

✦

Your ticket to Six Flags.

*They're better
than you expect them to be
at jigsaw puzzles.*

✦

Pop Rocks are back on the market!

✦

*They don't look all that bad
when their hair is unbrushed.*

✦

Giving a kid a flashlight
will inspire him to read more.

*A kid is never embarrassed
to wear green on St. Patrick's Day,
even if he's not Irish.*

◆

A kid can sit on your lap
if there's not enough room.

◆

*You could probably learn
how to hypnotize yourself
by watching your child
rock back and forth
on an infant swing.*

You can make
little boys wear sandals.

✦

*You have never laughed
until you've watched
a ballet class
for four-year-olds.*

✦

You have never cried
until you've watched
your child
graduate from high school.

Most children
throw up in public
only once in their lives.

✦

It really is the teacher's job
to teach them,
not yours.

✦

The first time your child reads
"The Gift of the Magi,"
he or she will be blown away
by the ending.

249

Adorable in feet pajamas.

✦

They'll share at least
the green Life Savers
and black jelly beans
with you.

✦

All those bridesmaids' dresses
you never wore again
make nice costumes
for your children now.

There's no evidence that
those D.A.R.E. programs work,
so feel free
to stay home
if your child's school sponsors one.

✦

All your kids'
best character traits
were inherited from you.
All their worst ones
came from your spouse.

*They'd much rather hear
about the stork
than have you tell them
the horrible truth.*

✦

Children are very conscientious
about letting you know
when their siblings
have done something wrong.

✦

*Kids give you something to talk about
with your in-laws.*

Once you have children,
you quickly jettison
the unreasonably high standards
you formerly held.

✦

Admit it:
you love all that
American Girl stuff.

✦

Taking your kids to
Discovery Zone gives you a great
chance to catch up on your reading.

You're much less
self-conscious about
saying poop *now, aren't you?*

✦

They honestly think
being older is better.

✦

Though you'd never dream *of*
subjecting her to that life,
your daughter really could
make it as a teen model.

Kids don't care
if the house is a mess.

✦

With the elementary-school set,
the song
"YMCA"
never, ever goes out of style.

✦

There's always a crayon around
when you want to
jot down a phone number.

*Your child may grow up
to be a criminal,
but at least
he will not grow up to be
Jerry Springer.*

✦

Unlike a spouse,
a child can sleep
through your snoring.

✦

*They accept the results of
"scissors, paper, rock" as final.*

You can actually
give a child a merrier Christmas
by working less hard
to make Christmas perfect.

✦

*To a five-year-old,
you are a billionaire.*

✦

Babies can put their toes
in their mouths—
not necessarily a great thing,
but who else can do it?

If it hadn't been for toddlers,
skid-proof socks
never would have been
invented.

✦

Babies work much harder
to get exercise
than adults do.

✦

They take a better nap
after their
Tumbling Tykes class.

PRODUCTS WE'D LIKE TO SEE

Time-Release Barney:
Limits your child's exposure to the singing purple dinosaur and his p.c. little friends. Made by the folks who brought you the V-chip.

Microscopic Top-Drawer Cameras:
Photographs contents of drawer in a continuous loop. Detects condoms, plastic bags filled with drugs, letters from last summer's boyfriend or girlfriend. So tiny your teen will never find it.

Ennui Night-Light:
Plug in this little light with sound, and your child will fall asleep immediately as he listens to *The Collected Speeches of Michael Dukakis.* Also comes in *Public Television Pledge Week* (654 minutes), *The Instruction Manual for the Oki Data OL 400E Printer* (452 minutes), and *Table Manners Explained* (endless).

Disappearing Band-Aids:
For those kids who think their ensemble is not complete without full bandage mufti, these Band-Aids fade away as soon as the mild mishap that caused them to be put on in the first place is forgotten.

*Children live
in blissful ignorance
of the diseases
that may later kill them.*

✦

The ring bearer
gets *way* more attention
than the groom.

✦

*A baby rarely grasps
the similarity between
a playpen and jail.*

Kids as consumers
add billions of dollars
to the economy.

✦

*Babies like to "read,"
even if the book
is upside down.*

✦

You can train them
to think
that soda is a treat.

*A kid singing off-key
is charming.*

✦

If your
dinner party is dull,
you can always
go check on the baby.

✦

*Kids think
it's a privilege
to get crutches.*

They can wear
horizontal stripes
without looking chunky.

✦

They're not pee-shy.

✦

They're above
such petty concerns
as who colors
Carolyn Bessette-Kennedy's hair.

Your child's
performance
in the school play
will never be
viciously parodied in
Forbidden Broadway.

✦

You wouldn't be able
to sleep if someone
was carrying you around,
but a baby can.

It's so sweet
the way
preschoolers
think they're helping
when they're really
getting in the way.

◆

Imagine a mind
so pure
and unfettered
that all it cares about
is what's for lunch.

To an infant,
your ugly bifocals
are grab-worthy jewels.

◆

No matter how bad a parent
you think you are,
there's always someone out there
who's worse.

◆

You can't accuse them
of not trying to dress themselves before
they're old enough to know how.

To a child,
the baggy skin under your arm
is fascinating.

✦

Counting
Massachusetts license plates
keeps a kid in a car
busy for a good hour.

✦

Only a two-year-old
can get away with a potbelly.

*Don't think twice
about leftovers.
The baby-sitter
will take care of them.*

◆

Letters from camp.

◆

*Having a kid
makes you think
you can write
children's books.*

Anyone who has a
kid younger than yours
likes you for the
potential hand-me-downs.

✦

*Is there anything sweeter
than tiny flip-flops?*

✦

If you didn't have kids,
you might not know
how funny
The Simpsons is.

*Casinos are very strict
about not letting kids gamble,
so there's no way
your twelve-year-old
can lose everything
on the slot machines.*

✦

A reason to buy shares of Kodak.

✦

*They won't need a face-lift
until they're old enough
to pay for it themselves.*

271

They consider
the airport shuttle bus
a fun part of the vacation.

✦

Patting a little boy's crew cut.

✦

If they're young enough,
they think they're
playing a video game
even though
they haven't put in
any tokens.

You can always count
on their letting you know
if you give them a present
they already have.

✦

They go barefoot
so much that the soles of their feet
become permanently durable.

✦

The invitation
to a child's birthday party
includes an ending time.

Having kids
gives you many more opportunities
to play air hockey.

◆

*They'd actually
find it distasteful
if you were hip.*

◆

As long as you
keep their closet door closed,
monsters will never eat
your children.

They don't mind
if their hair gets blown around
by the wind.

✦

They don't have wars—
just arguments
about whether
innies or outies are better.

✦

They don't mind it
when you ask them
about their private lives.

Go ahead—
use paper plates.

✦

They are beautiful merely
by virtue
of their youth.

✦

That adorable fluff
that newborns
call hair.

IT'S GREAT
TO BE A KID

No one makes fun of you
for being
pushed around
in a stroller.

✦

No one laughs
at your waist-high panties.

✦

Get to ride on your dad's shoulders
(whereas he doesn't
get to ride on *his* dad's shoulders).

Pigtails look cute on you.

Nursery school
is more fun
than having a job.

You don't have to carry keys.

Think of all the occasions
when overalls will do.

Eventually,
they let you cross the street.

Crying in public
without embarrassment

You can make money
selling lemonade
that your mother
bought in the first place.

✦

Allowance is not taxed
by the government.

✦

No alimony
or child-support payments.

✦

No one expects you
to shave your legs
until you hit your teens.

✦

Private car and driver.

Live-in cook.

✦

Inflation has put
your allowance
on a par with
Kathie Lee's garment workers.

✦

Don't need a winter dress coat.

✦

Complain excessively
and you may be served pizza
instead of pork loin.

✦

Getting into R-rated movies
while paying
under-twelve rates.

Instead of paying to join
an expensive health club,
you have phys. ed.

◆

Getting gym excuses
from the school nurse:
a victory
for the little people!

◆

They'll never give you
the death sentence
(though you might
get the time-out chair).

◆

If all else fails,
you can have a tantrum.

*They can't tell the difference
between expensive
Belgian chocolate
and Hershey's.*

✦

Young children
can marry
and divorce ad infinitum
and never pay alimony!

✦

*No inhibitions
when it comes to dancing.*

Once you have kids,
people stop nagging
you to have kids.

✦

After you've had one,
you know enough
not to let
the second one
do oil painting
in the living room.

✦

They don't get heartburn.

Pedialyte,

the magic elixir.

◆

Your daughter doesn't care

if another girl

at her birthday party

is wearing

the same dress.

◆

"Who's got your nose?"

works once or twice.

You can always tell
when they're lying,
even if you can't do
anything about it.

✦

Taking
a fifteen-year-old baby-sitter home
is sort of like
going on a date, isn't it?

✦

You can always try Ritalin.

Having a daughter
ensures that your telephone
will never break
through lack of use.

◆

Kids tend to know
a lot about sharks,
for some reason.

◆

Being a parent
gives you more chances
to impulse-buy.

Improve your vocabulary
by helping them prepare
for the SATs.

✦

According to other parents,
your surly offspring
is an absolute joy
at their houses.

✦

Having a busy teenager
helps you rehearse
the empty-nest syndrome.

*Your teenage son
can reach the top shelves
for you.*

✦

Those stick-on earrings
look pretty realistic.
So do those
fake nose rings.
Maybe you can
fob them off
on your child.

*Even stores
without public rest rooms
will let your child
use the bathroom.*

✦

They're
gratifyingly delighted
when you break down
and let them
do something
you've always forbidden.

Until they're eight,
it doesn't hurt too much
if they hit you.

✦

When your teenager
flounces around the house
insulting you, at least you know
she's safe at home.

✦

That moment they see you
after a whole day apart
and their eyes light up.

They won't
stand you up
for lunch.

✦

Although they fall a lot,
they rarely
break a hip.

✦

Correcting
their mispronunciations
makes you feel
so educated.

There's nothing more liberating
than peeling off a
Snugli
on a hot day.

✦

When they're not tattling on
or hurting one another,
children like to play together.

✦

Thanks to calculators,
the younger generation
doesn't need math.

Freeze juice
in ice-cube trays
for a (sort of) quick
and (sort of) tasty treat!

✦

Little kids
brim with old-fashioned respect
for big kids.

✦

A house with children
is more likely to be a house
with up-to-date smoke detectors.

*Kids give you a reason
to make a will . . .
and one of these days
you'll get around to it.*

✦

Most of them
are good sports
about audience participation.

✦

*They think it's a privilege
pressing the buttons
on the cash machine.*

You'll have
tons of fun
on that
Brownie jamboree
once
you resign yourself
to not getting any sleep
all night long.

✦

You'll be an instant expert
during the brief period
that your son is interested
in Superman's childhood.

From zero to ten,
a girl really needs only a pair
of white tights
and Mary Janes for any party.

✦

Remember how funny it was
when the goat ate your belt
at the petting zoo?

✦

They won't notice
if you hem their clothes and
"sew on" their Brownie badges
with a glue gun.

HOW TO END AN ARGUMENT WITH A KID

"Because I said so."

✦

"When you're a parent,
you can stay up past ten
on a school night."

✦

"When I was your age . . ."

✦

" A _____ is not a toy."

"If your friends
jumped off a cliff,
would you jump off one, too?"

♦

"You have an answer
for everything,
don't you?"

♦

"Fine.
Then the family won't go
on vacation tomorrow."

♦

"Would you like me
to stop the car
and let you out
right here?"

"John, I have a life, too."

◆

"Do I look
like I have three hands?"

◆

"I'll let your father
deal with this
because I can't possibly."

◆

"Great.
Now you've
made your mother cry."

◆

"Tomorrow."

"You're aware, aren't you,
that Great-Aunt Nellie
is not going to be around forever?"

"You made me sorry
I chose
to become a parent
instead of getting
my master's."

"All I can say is,
your sister would never act like that."

"If you don't hurry,
I'll leave you here."

"You're absolutely right."

For a child,
setting up the checkerboard
is half the fun of playing.
Make that
two-thirds of the fun.

◆

Your kids
are the only people
who might possibly
have an interest
in your family tree—
and even there,
the chance is slim.

*You'll be surprised
at how useful it is
to own an encyclopedia*

✦

Having young children
gives you a good chance
to try to stop
swearing so much.

✦

*When they're little,
they're proud to belong to the
same political party as you.*

302

Liver isn't as healthy
as our parents believed,
so you never need
to force your child to eat it.

✦

Someone else
will be den leader
if you hold out long enough.

✦

Threatening to sign your kids up
for an etiquette course
may get them to sit up straight.

Threatening
to move
to a new house
may get them to clean up
their rooms.

✦

Of *course* you have to watch them
like a hawk
when you're at the beach,
but it's nice to know
the lifeguard is watching, too.

In a pinch,
a baby can sleep
in a drawer.

✦

When they're learning to talk,
you can train them
to call your enemies names like
Dork and Saggy—then claim,
"She just came up with it
on her own!"

When they ask you to explain
New Yorker *cartoons,*
it reminds you how urbane
and sophisticated you are.

◆

In some states, you are allowed
to pinch your children's tushes
until the age of eleven.

◆

Easy laughers.

You finally feel like a grown-up.

✦

*They don't look
like cheap whores
when they wear
mules, chipped nail polish,
and animal prints.*

✦

Always willing to cheat
on behalf of the team.

*Will consider going to the store
to buy you stuff, just because it means
you're letting them go
to the store by themselves.*

✦

They're just so . . . well preserved!

✦

*Considers eating cold cereal
for dinner a special treat.*

✦

Can crawl into teeny-weeny spaces
to stick plugs back in the wall.

If only the secretary of state
could resolve international crises
by counting to three!

◆

A pinch of glitter
goes a long, long way.

◆

Who else can you teach
that formula thing about cricket chirps
and thunderstorms?

◆

They can sled forever.

Even when you're mad at them,
you still want to
kiss them good night.

✦

Their worst enemy—the deadly
Tyrannosaurus rex
—has been extinct
for millions of years.

✦

Their clothes don't take up
a lot of closet space.

They bite only
until they're three or four.

✦

Who else can draw a picture of God?

✦

Dazzle them
by daring to swat at a bee
with your bare hand!

✦

*Toddlers are innately good
at interpretive dance.*

It's possible that the reason
your kid is flunking
the second grade
is because he's just too smart
and unchallenged.

✦

*They're good with
mindless tasks, like stirring.*

✦

Children give you
and your spouse
something to fight about.

*How about
those grandchildren?*

◆

Kids dominate the conversation,
which comes in useful
sometimes.

◆

*You can give each kid up to
$10,000 tax-free a year.*

◆

A form of immortality.

*They love
taking pictures,
even if there's no film
in the camera.*

✦

Children
make you appreciate
the sound of silence.

✦

*They like icing
out of the can better.*

Awww!
They're precious
when they're asleep.

✦

Someone to tell you—
honestly
—you're too old to wear that.

✦

You don't have to teach them
the facts of life—
they learned it all
on the.bus.

All those child prodigies
that your kid is not—
they usually end up
failures as adults.

◆

Kids really *do* say the darndest things.